List 5 things you like about yourself:

Write a newspaper clipping about your achievements:

Complete the sentence: "I deserve happiness because...":

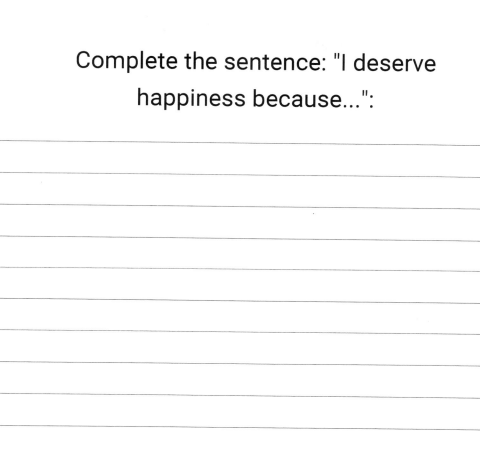

List 5 things you're memorable for:

Write 3 compliments you have heard from others:

_____

_____

_____

_____

_____

_____

_____

_____

_____

_____

_____

_____

_____

_____

_____

_____

_____

_____

_____

_____

_____

_____

_____

Think of the nicest thing anyone has ever said to you. List it below:

List 5 physical features you like about yourself:

Consider your role model, and jot down 3 qualities you share with them:

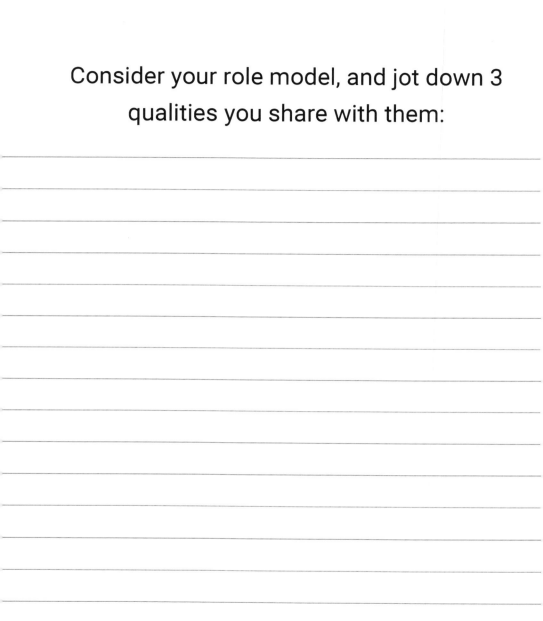

Jot down 20 things that make you smile:

_____
_____
_____
_____
_____
_____
_____
_____
_____
_____
_____
_____
_____
_____
_____
_____
_____
_____
_____
_____

Write about a positive achievement of yours that you didn't think you could achieve at the time:

Describe a positive change you made to your life in the last year:

List 5 words you like reading:

List 4 things you would like to achieve in the next 24 hours:

_____

_____

_____

_____

_____

_____

_____

_____

_____

_____

_____

_____

_____

_____

_____

_____

_____

_____

_____

_____

_____

Complete the sentence: "This month will be amazing because I...":

Describe a thing you look forward to when you wake up:

List your 5 favorite smells:

Jot down what you would do in the next 24 hours if you could eliminate fear:

Write about a song you could listen to on repeat, and why you like it so much:

Write down a forgiveness to yourself for something you feel guilty about:

Complete the sentence: "My friends love me because I..":

List out your victories from the past week:

Write down some lyrics that you identify with:

Write about something you're currently afraid of, then write what you think it would take to overcome that fear:

Describe or draw what you can see out of the window:

Complete the sentence: "I make a positive contribution to the world because I...":

Write about a person who helps or supports you positively:

Write about your favorite piece of clothing and how you feel when you are wearing it:

Write a lonely hearts ad as if it were someone looking for you:

Answer this: I deserve happiness because...:

_____
_____
_____
_____
_____
_____
_____
_____
_____
_____
_____
_____
_____
_____
_____
_____
_____
_____
_____
_____

Write about your favorite food and why you love eating it:

List 6 things you would love to receive from someone:

Explain who your favorite tv character is, and why you like them so much:

_____
_____
_____
_____
_____
_____
_____
_____
_____
_____
_____
_____
_____
_____
_____
_____
_____
_____
_____
_____

Complete the sentence: the next 24 hours will be amazing if I...":

_____

_____

_____

_____

_____

_____

_____

_____

_____

_____

_____

_____

_____

_____

_____

_____

_____

_____

_____

_____

Sit in silence with your eyes closed. At the end of the time, jot down what you thought of during that time:

Describe a time you laughed so hard you almost couldn't breathe:

Describe a time you felt truly loved:

Write a thank you letter to your body:

Write a thank you letter to your brain:

Write about a small task that you've been putting off, go do it, then write down how you feel when you complete it:

Describe the place that makes you feel most relaxed:

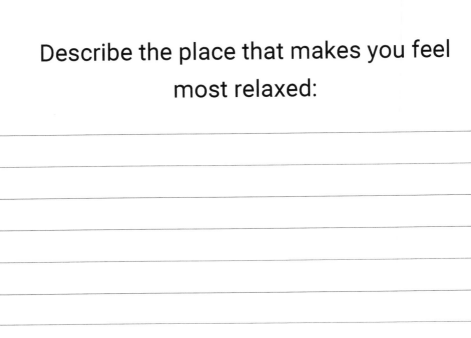

Complete the sentence: "I deserve love because...":

_____
_____
_____
_____
_____
_____
_____
_____
_____
_____
_____
_____
_____
_____
_____
_____
_____
_____
_____
_____

List 3 things you do that give back to the world:

- PICK UP LITTER

Pay a compliment to someone, then document here how it made you feel:

_____

_____

_____

_____

_____

_____

_____

_____

_____

_____

_____

_____

_____

_____

_____

_____

_____

_____

_____

Organize your desk, bookcase, or other small space, then document here how it made you feel:

_____

_____

_____

_____

_____

_____

_____

_____

_____

_____

_____

_____

_____

_____

_____

_____

_____

_____

_____

_____

_____

_____

_____

_____

_____

Complete the sentence: "I am looking forward to...":

_____

_____

_____

_____

_____

_____

_____

_____

_____

_____

_____

_____

_____

_____

_____

_____

_____

_____

List out 10 places you would love to visit one day:

Write or draw a broadway poster for a show about your life, starring you. Include reviews:

List 5 things you consider yourself knowledgable about:

Describe something that fascinates you:

Describe a time that you were good with money:

_____
_____
_____
_____
_____
_____
_____
_____
_____
_____
_____
_____
_____
_____
_____
_____
_____
_____
_____
_____
_____

List the highlights of the past week:

Jot down 15 things that excite you:

List 3 foods you would love to try one day:

Sketch or describe the room around you:

Write your name vertically down the
page, and then write out a positive
attribute for each letter (e.G. H is for
happy):

List 3 things you do that make you feel calm and peaceful:

Sketch or describe your 'happy place':

Write about your favorite time of day and why you like it so much:

Write about the best thing you ever received in the mail:

Complete the sentence: "My life deserves more...":

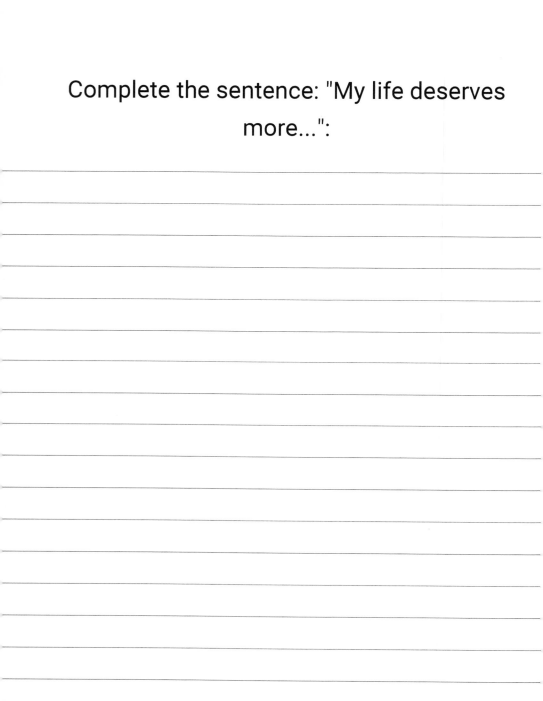

List 6 things you are most proud of:

Describe your ideal morning:

List 3 short term goals you have:

Explain a lesson you learned this week, and how you will implement it moving forwards:

Write down 3 pieces of advice for your future self:

Write about an interesting person you met in the last year:

Write about a time you conquered a fear:

Describe the career of your dreams:

List 3 movies that make you feel happy:

Explain your favorite weather, including a memory you have during that weather:

_____

_____

_____

_____

_____

_____

_____

_____

_____

_____

_____

_____

_____

_____

_____

_____

_____

_____

_____

_____

_____

Write about a good habit you want to develop:

_____
_____
_____
_____
_____
_____
_____
_____
_____
_____
_____
_____
_____
_____
_____
_____
_____
_____
_____

Complete the sentence: "People have me to thank for...":

- Scott Todd: approachability of supervisor

Describe or sketch out the last photo you took:

Write down five positive traits you have, and next to them write the name of a person you admire who shares that trait:

Write about a skill you have that you would like to teach to others:

Write about a recent gift you gave someone:

Describe a reoccuring dream you have:

Complete the sentence: "I can reward myself tomorrow by...":

Summarize the last positive phone or online conversation you had with someone:

Describe what activities you would do if you could take a "Wellbeing day" tomorrow:

Write about something you are saving up for:

- RV

Describe your perfect social event:

Write about the person you consider to be your best friend, and explain why you love them:

Consider the colors that define happiness and use only those colors to write or draw freely on this page:

Complete the sentence: "I am grateful that I have...":

Explain what you would like to learn if time, money, and effort were not a factor:

Close your eyes and write down 10 things you love about yourself, embrace the uncertainty of not seeing what you are writing:

Explain who the one person you feel most comfortable around is:

Describe or draw the last amazing meal you ate:

Explain one thing you changed in your life that improved things for you:

Write a book blurb for your life story:

_____

_____

_____

_____

_____

_____

_____

_____

_____

_____

_____

_____

_____

_____

_____

_____

_____

_____

_____

Describe your favorite photo of yourself:

Complete the sentence: "I am excited for...":

_____

_____

_____

_____

_____

_____

_____

_____

_____

_____

_____

_____

_____

_____

_____

_____

_____

_____

Write down 7 things you own that bring you happiness:

Write down 3 things you have given to others that bring them happiness:

_____

_____

_____

_____

_____

_____

_____

_____

_____

_____

_____

_____

_____

_____

_____

_____

_____

_____

_____

_____

_____

Describe your favorite cup or mug, explain why you like it more than other cups or mugs:

Describe your favorite thing to feel under your feet (e.G. Sand, grass, carpet), and document some places where you can feel that:

List 4 ways you have recently been proactive:

List 5 things you have learned about yourself while completing this journal:

Explain what steps you plan to take next to continue helping yourself live your best life:

_____
_____
_____
_____
_____
_____
_____
_____
_____
_____
_____
_____
_____
_____
_____
_____
_____
_____
_____
_____
_____
_____
_____
_____

Made in the USA
Columbia, SC
06 June 2020